3 in 1: Business, Marketing & Technology

Exploiting the Struggles of Small Business

Brandon Sims

Copyright © 2019 Brandon Sims

All rights reserved. No part of this publication may be reproduced, stored in a retrieval system, or transmitted in any form or by any means, electronic, mechanical, photocopying, recording, or otherwise, without written permission of the publisher, except by reviews who may quote brief passages in a review.

First published, 2019

Front cover photograph by Free Voyage Photography
Book design by Brandon Sims

DEDICATION

To all the school teachers and professors that I have encountered over the many years of education. Listening to all the many questions I've had, but willing to consider them. Thank you!

ACKNOWLEDGMENT

Thank you to my friends and family for the continued support and guidance, every adventure and memory is what was able to make this possible.

Most notably, to my parents who have taught me the value of money and to continue pursuing forward in challenges. Especially, my father who allowed me to take the reins on various projects at the golf range to develop solutions and solve the problems.

God Bless!

CONTENTS

Acknowledgments i

1 How It Begins 1
2 Business Development 3
3 Marketing to The Masses 11
4 Technology Invasion 17
5 All Together 23

1
HOW IT BEGINS

At the end of junior year in high school, I could not focus on my school work. I could only solely imagine about the potential of business opportunities during the forthcoming summer. This distraction stemmed from growing up around a family-owned small business golf driving range. At a young age, I exclusively held the position of cashier, sharpening my math and customer service skills. From there, I was promoted to assistant general manager within a few years, where I was tasked to defuse incidents and maintain the highest quality of customer service. After supporting those responsibilities for many years, I created my current position as Director of Technology, in 2012, where I have the wonderful opportunity to introduce technology at the golf range, promote what makes the facility unique and engage with customers.

By now, you are probably noticing this is a constantly developing story and a long time coming. It is all true. This adventure most certainly allowed me to encounter a vast array of challenges and successes, including being fired countless times on Saturday and re-hired the following Monday. This was predominantly due to my developing age of 12 years old, at the time. Although this unfortunate consistency occurred, it is also what drove me searching to understand the operations of the business to best serve the clients and the business.

A considerable amount of time has passed, nearly twenty years, since I began working at the golf range and in the golf industry. Across all those years there have been countless situations that have required diligence, understanding, and praise in the highest order to make it a success.

Through this book, I intend to share not only personal stories of this wonderful adventure through business but dive deeper into the discussion of business and the various aspects of marketing, and technology, which are found entangled with each other.

2
BUSINESS DEVELOPMENT

A small business can potentially have its challenges in getting started and maintaining operations, although there are also huge benefits to starting and operating a business. Whether you are single, married or have kids the opportunities can practically be endless for any type of business.

With starting a business, picking a name is probably the first most challenging decision, besides deciding to start the business. In this process of picking a business name, there are a few steps that I suggest following. Begin with brainstorming catchy words, that expresses some meaning, and are potentially related to the industry. Secondly, complete an internet search to see if those names are available. This online search can encompass your state's corporate commission and even cross-checking with domain name databases. Finally, you want to ensure you enjoy the name.

Thinking ahead about legally protecting the longevity of the business and personally protect yourself there are a few options while maintaining the integrity of the business. While there's paperwork and cost involved to incorporate the business, having financial separation from your personal belongs is worth the cost. Forming a Limited Liability Company (LLC) achieves this goal by keeping all profit and losses within the business. I would heed a warning towards forming a partnership as the legal parameters that ensure both parties uphold their duties is next to null. To put this into practice, a good rule of thumb is when you get married that is your partner, for life, which then makes it a challenge to have a second partner a part of a business deal.

To gain a better understating of incorporation options I would encourage you to consult with an accountant and attorney.

Conversely, not saying that all business adventures will be successful, it requires a mixture of passion and drive. Over my long tenure, all the situations and discussions in business have been centered around four prominent categories of financial, industry and business principles which all are contributing factors to managing and developing the business.

Financial Aspects

One of the top reasons that people decide to get into business is to make money and if that isn't the reason, then the argument can be made that it takes money to operate. If the business doesn't have money or is in debt then, the end is near. It has been said that most startups will not last past their third year, simply because of financial issues. Thus, at the end of the day having a financial understanding is vital for the start, operation, and continuing of any business, non-profit or for-profit.

A popular saying "get rich quick" is extremely catchy, but is untrue, thus take the time and slow down to gauge the business environment and economy around you. This is a very easy scenario to get trapped in, whether receiving a marketing proposal or pursuing a business opportunity.

I will be the first to say that, "I am not perfect with money", however, to overcome this shortcoming I have principles in place to guide me on financial decisions. Unfortunately, from time to time, my desires take over and disregard those principles. This is when having a trusted person to bounce financial scenarios off; such as a friend, parent, or spouse. This concept is comparable to the checks and balances of the US Government, except you make the final say, so it provides an opportunity to think aloud.

I would encourage you to dive deeper and reflect on some financial principles for you to incorporate into your organization. There are several organizations and individuals who provide financial education and resources, including Financial Peace University and Crown Financial.

With this critical understanding of how finances both play a role and require diligence in handling their decisions in business put forth, there are several reasonable business practices from the perspective of financial stability. These financial practices can help start and maintain the financial status of the organization.

- Aim to be debt-free
- Complete work in house
- Buy used
- Make profit centers

Out of all my years working at the golf range, if I have learned one thing being debt-free is the best feeling to achieve. While it is the best feeling, being debt-free can also be one of the most difficult principles to achieve initially. This challenge of being debt-free and starting a business derives from the fact that it takes money to get a business running. Therefore, if cash isn't on hand to get the business off the ground, a "micro-loan" is an option for initial investment allowing the business to increase cash on hand. Again, for this specific area of conversation, I encourage you to speak with an accountant to understand the ramifications of taking on debt.

Adding to the debt can create a snowball effect, thus as time goes on it is harder to get out of debt. Therefore, turning this scenario around, the benefit of increased cash on hand leads to the capability to pay off all debt that is owed and will diminish the external pressures from lenders on you. Not saying you cannot use credit cards. Although, I do encourage you to pay the monthly balance and consider the expenditures during purchases. The feeling that you are "exclusively working for someone else" is removed as the revenue and interest on the principle can be kept and saved, versus paid out to cover the debt. As the achievement is maintained you will notice an abundance more of freedom financially. However, to maintain that status, audit the businesses resource list and look at ways that cost can be reduced, while not interfering with quality too much. One way that we were able to reduce cost at the golf range was by completing work in house and purchasing in bulk.

Every business has a unique building and surrounding environment. Even so, there's always a laundry list of projects to complete. While there may be some projects that are well out of your skillset, that can still leave plenty of opportunities to complete some projects in house.

The evaluation of determining whether to outsource a project depends on the answer to a few questions: Is it a project that you're capable of doing? Will you save more money on the supplies than not outsourcing? Do you have the resources to do the project? If you answered, "Yes" to at least one question then consider completing the project in house. Being a golf range, the biggest project that we complete in house is mowing the facility, there's twenty acres of land to mow every week, which saves us tens of thousands of dollars monthly.

As you approach the possibility of completing a project in-house, the best recommendation is to complete cost analysis for doing the project in comparison to outsourcing the project. It is best to get a quote from if possible three vendors to compare with. Over time, it will become an instantaneous response of, "In-house!"

Expanding from completing projects in house, there becomes times within reason purchasing used equipment is beneficial. As a golf range, we were frequently purchasing and laminating seasonal signs. As time went on, we foresaw an increase of signs purchasing on the horizon. So, we researched the options of purchasing a vinyl cutter to make professional vinyl signs in house. The cost of a new vinyl cutter was out of our budget, but we did not stop looking, instead, we considered a slightly used vinyl cutter. After diligently looking online, we located an excellent barely used vinyl cutter for half the price. Six years later that vinyl cutter is still rolling along and has cut hundreds of yards of vinyl lettering and shapes. While in return saving us thousands of dollars of having to work with a sign company.

When looking to buy used, the unprecedented need is maintaining the quality and integrity of the product or service being offered. Evaluate the equipment or resource that you require and perhaps purchasing used will fit the need.

What are your current profit centers?

Keep in mind, business is centered around providing a service or good, this can be taken one more step, to provide a need or a want. The concept of a profit center is a segment of your business that exclusively generates revenue from one activity. The primary service or good that your business offers is your first profit center. In addition to this, by adding other services or goods form additional profit centers and expand the arm of influence in the surrounding market. The bottom line is the more profit centers, which typically support the primary aspect of business, the greater the business's revenue stream is.

Dive into the industry

With a financial foundation set for the flow of money, understanding the industry that you are in improves the success of the business. Although, every industry is unique various facets can carry over, whether operating a retail space or service; operating a golf range, gym, restaurant, being a car mechanic or plumber. Evaluating your industry allows you to identify services and goods that can be offered to your clients. This evaluation sets up the research phase for opportunities, for them to be discussed about the benefit to growth and development of the business.

This is a great time to review the procurement suppliers that are in your supply chain. It is, "OK", if they all are directly correlated to your industry. However, do not be afraid to reach out to vendors out of the industry to fulfill orders. By looking at vendors outside of your industry, it allows for new ideas and concepts to consider that can lower your expenditures and increase customer satisfaction.

A prime example of looking outside of the industry was several years back customers were requesting cup holders on the tee line. After months of research and sample reviews, I settled on a boat marine supplier as a product was identifying the would be durable and embodied longevity to the outdoor elements.

Furthermore, every year my father and I aim to visit between two to six golf ranges, typically as we travel on vacation (usually going to see family), doing so allows us to gain, share, and discuss new ideas for the business.

> Listen to clients about improvements

An effortless idea that has stemmed from one of those trips was adding a sign at each tee box on the golf range, identifying the yardage to the five target greens in the field. This simple addition originally overlooked for several years has received many compliments because it is a useful aid for clients. As for the golf industry, identifying yardage is a critical part of the golf game.

These examples demonstrate the benefit of understanding the industry to best serve the client and the business. In reviewing your industry keep in mind a few organizations in the industry may offer something that you do not, this doesn't necessarily mean that your business must offer the exact services or goods. This correlates to the financial aspect of the business as those extended services or goods may not suit the region that you are located in. This is a reasonable understanding, even though it just may be the same regional, national or global industry, there are select aspects that are not as receptive by your clients in your region.

A useful piece of information to assist navigating the marketplace is by identify whether your business is a necessity or a luxury. Once you identify the importance that your business is to your clients it extrapolates how to best serve your clients and market to them. This especially, becomes useful as the economy shifts and new products are introduced into your industry.

Ethics drive the message

Every business is required is make decisions, in doing so values, morals and ethics are displayed. From this, the treatment of clients and potentially bad situations can be resolved.

As a public facility, in the environment we have clients aging from two years old to seventy-five years old. Because of this, we have set a policy precedent not to sell or allow alcohol on the premise. Periodically, there's an adult client that brings an alcoholic beverage onto the facility. When an employee finds out of this situation, we merely inform the client of the policy and request them to throw it away. At which point, 99% of the time the client complies. Which we are thankful for. On the other hand, the remaining 1% of situations tend to escalate a little. Certainly, while some issues aren't worth fighting over it does depend on the reaction of the client on when to step away and allow the situation to calm down.

But, how would you handle it? You may not initially know, although having a predefined guideline makes for fewer decisions in those moments. So, where do those notions derive from?

Ultimately, those notions of how to react during a situation stem first from values. Values can be divided into two categories: personal and transferable. The personal values are where we as individuals find meaning and guidance as decisions are being made. As a business is starting or being developed there are values that are transferred from our personal values. These transferable values set the foundation of the purpose, and actions that the business will make.

Those values will determine the important areas for the business to stand for and will reflect into the ethics. While ethics is often the difference of what is right or wrong, legal or illegal, it is the style that the business will carry its self and use to set forth the business policies.

Caring for clients

The idea of how the business is engaging and caring for clients has been briefly touched on, although it is the final piece of setting the business in the direction of success. While this topic is often the hardest for a business owner to hear, it is a connecting piece for marketing to be worthy of financing.

Fundamentally, this section calls for a self-reflection of processes, systems and the business appeal to clients. No matter the business type or industry there are processes and systems in place that engage with clients. Those systems should be simplified to ease the confusion of clients and streamlined to speed the process up. At which point, employees should be educated in the processes and systems in place.

With the systems solidified employees should be able to reasonably complete tasks to client satisfaction. With the adjustments made from this reflection, customers will feel attended to and turn into repeat business.

At the golf range, we evaluated the quality of materials that were being used such as the golf balls. Keep in mind that this is a product that every client interacts with. After receiving feedback from various clients, we decided to upgrade our golf balls from a one-piece ball to a two-piece ball. This decision was more expensive for us to acquire, however, the better equipment allowed for greater performance by our clients and provided an enhanced experience while practicing their golf swing.

****

Even with the growing use of technology, the business field still operates on many of the same principles of decades ago. This stands true because of universal acceptance and understanding. It takes money to operate a business and clients to spend money with the business. This incredible cycle develops and forms a powerful relationship between the business and the client. The business can exist for more than selling products and services but standing for and with something.

3
MARKETING TO THE MASSES

Many people say, "marketing is the most vital aspect for business success". While they may have a point for the importance that marketing plays in business, I believe it is equally vital as the other two areas being discussed. Whether, "marketing" is an area of your passion or zero understanding, marketing assists to bring clients through the doors of the business. The popular saying, "build it and they will come" misses a vital fact of informing the community of the business's existence and providing an excellent product.

To overcome this slight dilemma, the use of a marketing strategy puts forth the road map of representing the business to the public. The marketing strategy can be completed in three steps, SAS: Specify, Action, Set.

First, specify an issue you would like to resolve or information that should be known about the business. Second, make an action that clients can do. Lastly, set a time frame for the action to be achieved within.

The marketing strategy supports what is known as the marketing mix (aka 4 Ps of marketing): product, price, place, and promotion. All decisions of marketing and business can be reflected in the marketing mix. The product category focuses on the solutions available for customers. The price category drives the discussion of the cost of the services and goods for customers. While the place category looks at the ease of access for customers

What are your 4 Ps?

to the business. Lastly, the promotion category promotes the discussion of the services and goods with customers.

There are several areas of marketing, especially in this growing day of digitalization, which have the potential to benefit the business when carefully considered and implemented.

Periodically, in operating a small business the marketing budget comes down to "best of breed". Essentially, this theory is identifying the areas in marketing for advertising that are least cost bearing, often the free opportunities are the most beneficial. This is a valuable theory as small businesses have limited funds available for advertising.

There are times when marketing campaigns cannot be measured for its success rate and "word of mouth" is one of those. This is merely because "word of mouth" is an organic action that will occur whether good or bad. Nonetheless, "word of mouth" out drives any other form of advertising and can't be controlled. I say that as a small scare tactic to mean, good advertising derives from good business practices.

Over the years of managing the marketing account at the golf range, the best advertising that was experienced was with free marketing. The highest engagement that occurred year after year was from a coupon fundraising booklet published by a regional organization. For this endeavor, we offered a "small basket of balls with a purchase", while in return the coupon booklet was helping various organizations in the community.

When evaluating marketing options, the decision should pass through a series of small tests. First and foremost, does the organization have a financial standing to afford the advertisement? Is the salesman being pushy? Often, the statement of "it's a hot deal" or "exclusive pricing" is used to entice a quicker purchase of the advertisement. In return, this sales ploy becomes a get rich quick for the salesman with little to no return for your organization.

Business Website

Having a website for the business is the greatest online presence that can exist, with uncountable benefits. This is true whether it is an eCommerce or brick-and-mortar business.

Ultimately, a website is an exclusive opportunity to tell potential clients about the business.

Having a website provides a clean slate for you to explain the three W's: who, what, and why. On the website explain who your business is, what you offer, why you should be chosen.

When you are working through the three W's, start by making a list and pick out a handful of big descriptive words to showcase on the website. Do not just put a long list of bullets on the website of services and goods offered.

> The website is for the: Who, What & Why.

A great addition that can be made to a website is an eCommerce section. This new section can form another profit center, being able to sell gift certificates or products on your website.

Having a powerful website doesn't come just by looking at it. It develops by understanding the business and gauging what customers are looking for. Therefore, as time goes on update the website, keeping it fresh.

When considering how to implement a website the options vary in roles of your business involvement to the development and maintenance. As discussed in the previous chapter, an option is to outsource the development and maintenance of a website design company. While this option tends to be more expensive, it frees up time and allows for a professional-looking website. The second option is, may involve some more time although can be achieved on a low-cost budget, using a do-it-yourself website builder. There are numerous services available to build the business's website, while still achieving a professional-looking website and not requiring a high level of technical knowledge. Typically, at the end of the day it comes down to available time and technical knowledge of which option is chosen.

Social Media

While being debated the most disruptive forms of advertising, there are plenty of platforms to select from. Each platform provides its unique benefits, although there's a collective benefit of increased brand awareness, boosted conversation, and being placed next to your competitors.

Being on social media, whether Facebook Business, Twitter, Instagram, YouTube or Pinterest, leads to being on one more location that potential clients have an opportunity to see the business.

While the business is presently on these sites it opens the door to share about goods and services that your business offers.

> What social media platforms does your business have a presence on?

Social media is the second greatest location to engage with potential and current clients, being able to provide a sneak-peak of operations and new attractions.

The typical aspect of marketing on the various social media platforms is having the option to purchase ad space. A benefit of advertising on social media is with the integration of being digital some criteria and filters can be set to make the marketing dollars a little more valuable, such as being able to define a target audience and optimize the objective-based on the marketing strategy.

Business Directories

The concept of business directories isn't new (remember the phonebook?), although digitalizing them is. With the introduction of the internet the ability to publish your business information (aka PAWN): Phone Number, Address, Website, & Name within a category or region will increase the business's visibility online.

There are quite literally hundreds of online business directories, nevertheless, there are about a dozen primary directories that are predominantly used. Many of the popular directories are Google My Business, Yellowpages.com, Yelp, Foursquare, SuperPages, and Manta.

> Is your online directory listing's up to date?

A major benefit of these select directories is that they're free to publish your business onto. Beyond, those directories each industry typically has a handful more, look at local and national industry associations. Most of the time it doesn't require an official membership to the association to list your business if you operate in that industry. Of course, each directory offers a few different features, such as PAWN sharing, hours of operation, customer reviews, and business posting. All these features, when used, are great benefits to the business.

To give a fair warning, with the automation of the internet it is likely that your business already has a listing in a directory or two. That isn't a problem, simply go to that directory, claim it, and begin to manage the listing. When managing a listing ensure the PAWN information is up-to-date and several excellent photos that represent the business.

Email Marketing

From my experience, email marketing is the second-best form of marketing, right behind word of mouth. With that stressed, have email marketing in place and knowing how to use the platform can positively benefit the business.

Email marking technology solutions aren't difficult to comprehend but have their burdens to implement. While the benefits greatly outweigh the challenges that may exist, it is only fair to identify both sides. The challenges include the email service cost, content creation, and gaining new subscribers. While the benefits are having enhanced email metrics, most direct marketing, builds excitement, and establishes authority.

Benefits of Email Marketing	Challenges of Email Marketing
• Enhanced Email Metrics • Most Direct Marketing • Builds Excitement • Establishes Authority	• Email Service Cost • Content Creation • Gaining New Subscribers

The basis of email marking is securely collecting client's emails; either after finishing a job for them, entry into a raffle or a birthday club. Then, sending a welcome email, which is a great opportunity for you to say, "Thank you for joining our newsletter". To maintain engagement, it is best to periodically send out an email keeping your subscribers informed about your brand and what the business offers. Lastly, an excellent idea is to share a coupon in the email to encourage the recipient to revisit your business soon.

Many email marketing services offer an automated email solution. This solution allows for part of your email marketing to be put on autopilot with a series of emails that have been pre-established to be sent out at a pre-determined time lapse.

Newspaper/ Magazines

Who doesn't remember the newspaper as a kid? If you don't remember, it is an unfortunate lost piece of marketing. I combine the newspaper and magazine ad marketing opportunities because they both are non-digitalized formats of advertising. While, over the last decade, there has been a decrease in people subscribing to print media, the typical reason for using this method is as a wide net of potential clients that are not on the internet.

Although, taking out an ad in the print media may just fit your business needs. Before doing so, evaluate the ad cost, ad size, and potential viewership.

When determining the placement of which newspaper or magazine, evaluate the reach that the publication has. Most publications are distributed within a region or community.

****

From all these opportunities in marketing, I must share the biggest insight that I've gained. Yes, marketing involves some trials and errors to determine the marketing streams that work best for your business. Although, as I mentioned earlier in the chapter small businesses don't have an endless money pit. Thus, use discernment and evaluation of each marketing stream and advertising opportunity to determine what will fit your needs, while capitalizing on the non-costing opportunities. Through all this good advertising derives from good business practices.

4
TECHNOLOGY INVASION

The field of technology isn't a new concept to business; nevertheless, it is been modifying the landscape for decades. Although, the type of technology that's being adopted is shifting. The most prominent technology benefits an online presence, promotes automation, and customer relationships.

As touched on in the previous chapter, having an online presence greatly assists with this ever-increasing digital age. Whether it is being on social media, business directory, or a personal website the ability to locate the business increases. Developing the online presence may take time but focus on understanding the business and gauging on what customers are looking for.

A part of being present online is also going where the clients or potential clients are. That said, social media is a contributing technology to draw business in and maintain engagement with recurring clients.

Firsthand experience, having an online presence can positively benefit the bottom line. As seen at the golf range social media was used to keep clients updated and provide a behind the scenes year-round.

Technology has developed enough to having the capability of being able to offer automation. The implementation of automation is offered in various ways. While reviewing the applications of autonomous systems or services there are a few things to keep in mind: what is the impact of current operations, what is the cost to acquire, how will it benefit the client? There are a few unknowns of automation, however, creating a benefit and risk chart helps define those areas for your specific business.

Automation = time savings

In the early 2000's, the introduction of automatic ball dispensers came about in the golf industry, allowing our clients to use the facility at their convenience. This addition to our business model was simple by adding the sale of a micro-chip key, which allowed our clients to use the facility conveniently and at a discounted rate.

This is a prime example of new inventions that were developed in an industry that can assist in the business. When evaluating the adoption of the automatic ball dispenser the rate of return needed to be evaluated in comparison to the efficiency for the clients and the back of business operations. In this case, adopting this autonomous technology fit our business model.

> Don't buy technology because it looks cool, but that it's helpful

However, this isn't always the case. In 2018, we were approached by a vendor which manufactures golf mats that automate the tee-up process of the golf ball. After a demo and breaking down the cost analysis, there was an increase in expenditure and customer re-training with little return on this investment (ROI). Even though this technology looked cool, we had to say "No".

Because we turned that automatic golf mat offer down doesn't mean that we won't put the information in a file or continue looking for innovation. Over the years, there have been countless projects that I have encountered and had deep consideration for. Many of those projects were postponed due to the waiting for a better implementation, simply because the technology was premature. Adopting technology late doesn't necessarily mean you are behind the ball. As difficult as this is to believe, not all technology is immediately useful in all industries, although there can be different scales of technology to implement.

Below are seven primary forms of technology that are used in business, with real-world application scenarios.

Point-Of-Sale/ Cash Register/ Inventory System

A Point-Of-Sale (POS), aka digitized cash register, is the system that allows the business to accept payment and track transactions. However, a POS can do a lot more than a standard cash register. So, what is the difference? A cash register has the most basic functionalities to offer, ringing up sales, printing a receipt, and receiving cash, check or credit card as payment. However, an external credit card terminal is required to accept credit cards with a cash register. The ultimate benefit of using a cash register is the simplicity of the technology and the elimination of monthly operating costs.

Whereas, a POS system provides more advanced features and has a different cost framework. Many of the POS vendors allow for operation on a tablet or smartphone device, with the small addition of a card reader for credit card transactions. Some of the features that are capable of a POS system are inventory management, loyalty program tracking, commission & tips, and enhanced reporting.

The reoccurring monthly cost associated with a POS system is the biggest financial difference with a cash register. As both options will require refills of thermal receipt paper, as needed.

Computer Options

The digital age continues to evade the business landscape. Therefore, the requirement of having access to a desktop computer, laptop, or tablet to complete the work.

All three-computer options work for a business, however, keep in mind the workflow that you aim to achieve. A desktop computer will most probably be the highest performance option. Also, it allows for the choice of a monitor that fits your environment. Another option for your office is a laptop, which taunts the portability feature. Like a laptop, a tablet is growing in popularity for the compact size and weight. When considering a tablet, the capability of required software is limited to the apps that are in the perspectives tablet's app store. Also, a reminder that the common ports may require adaptors to be utilized.

Ultimately, I feel that the bigger decision to make when selecting a computer is the option of the operating system (OS). When deciding there are two prominent choices for an operating system, Windows OS or Mac OS X.

To be fair, I am a predominant Windows OS user. However, like most things there are some pros and cons to evaluate and weigh of both OS's. Moreover, this list isn't limited and isn't specific to your industry or need.

Windows OS	Mac OS X
• Computer tends to be cheaper • More compatible accessories • Compatible with more software	• 1 supplier (Apple) • Limited accessory options • Great for graphic design

Software Tools

In the category of software for your business, there are thousands of programs available. The available software will vary based on the OS that your business is using. Most prominently you'll need a processing package, such as Microsoft Office. Other software that you may need will be directly correlated to your industry or business systems.

When researching and preparing to procure software licenses there are two ways to proceed. The first being, you procure the software outright and you own it. Most typically this method doesn't provide software feature updates, but it depends on the software manufacturer. The second procurement option is paying a monthly or annual fee. While this method tends to be more expensive there are a few differences, access to new feature releases and team collaboration (depending on the software).

When putting software on the business computer systems try to keep it to only necessary software, doing so will increase the security of your system, by minimizing potential vulnerabilities.

Networking Capability

Having the ability to connect to the World Wide Web is a big resource in business. Even if your business doesn't rely on the internet to operate the capability to promote the business online, process credit card payments or access business data stored in the cloud.

The availability of public Wi-Fi is growing. Whether, stepping into a coffee shop, local bakery, or car mechanic the availability to connect to their Wi-Fi. While offering Wi-Fi as a free service at your location has its benefit of increasing onsite engagement and time spent at your business. There are concerns to be aware of when offering public Wi-Fi to get ahead of. Clients should not access the same network that the business's operations run on as it can lead to a potential breach of security, allowing a user to access sensitive data that is on the business's computers. Also, when setting up the second Wi-Fi network it should be protected by a captive portal for visitors to be able to gain access to the internet through. This way after a set amount of time the guest is required to sign back into the public Wi-Fi.

Telephone System

A telephone system for the business can truly be as simple or complex that you can imagine. Going with the traditional landline phone is the cheapest and simplest to hookup. An increasing popular system is Voice Over Internet Protocol (VOIP). VOIP allows phone calls to be completed over the internet, versus a landline. An added feature that is available with VOIP is an auto attendant and robust voice mailbox system. Over the last decade, those with a phone number have been bombarded with Robo-telemarketing calls. By implementing the auto attendant feature the reduction of fake calls getting through to your employees can be seen, allowing employees to stay productive.

Of Course, if you are looking to cut the cord or work remotely most of the time, then going with a wireless cell phone plan is an option as well.

A feature that is available amongst all these options it an answering machine. The implementation of an answering machine presents a professional stature when a customer calls and allows for information to be shared without an employee needing to be present. It's another way to inform customers if the business has adjusted hours. Just be sure to keep it updated.

Financial Accounting System

In business financial stability and understanding is extremely vital, thus the accounting system gets focused on. When considering an accounting system, while there are many options, the basic functionality is to ensure that your business can keep track of revenue and expenditures.

Most typically an accounting system is a software package, although, the offerings have changed in the last several years. You'll either have the have chosen to have an accounting system stored locally on your computer system or in the cloud.

Customer Relationship Management Systems (CRM)

Every business has clients and customers, while some are one-time clients, but the vast majority are repeat business. Having a CRM promotes the relationships and interactions with clients by centralizing their information into one location. CRM typically supports a variety of core features: contact management, interaction tracking, email integration, quote management, and reporting. While not all CRM incorporating all those features, it will be a mixer of them and possibly even more.

The CRM may incorporate more functionality than others or your business may not require the assistance that it offers. CRM email marketing would be the most useful option; as it is a singular main feature and powerful promoting business tool.

While the concept of data isn't limited to the field of technology but expands throughout business operations; as data is collected and often stored with the assistance of technology. Specifically, the discussion of personal identifiable information (PII), which is a range of data that is associated with a person. PII includes full name, social security number, credit card numbers, and address. By identifying PII data and storing it in a secure location it can keep you compliant, with for example Payment Card Industry Data Security Standard (PCI DSS). While also protecting the information of your clients.

****

Technology can be a useful tool in the modern era, so long that it doesn't distract from the purpose and goals that the business has set forth. That same cautions are a warning to ensure that the technology improves customer service quality without diminishing it through distractions. As described in the seven primarily forms of technology that business uses, some applications may not suit your industry or specific business more than others. As a man once told me, "technology costs" therefore evaluate whether it will be helpful to the business's profitability in comparison to operating cost.

This goes hand in hand of having the latest and greatest technology isn't necessary. Therefore, adopting technology after it is been tested by the market is a reasonable reaction.

5
ALL TOGETHER

Business is exciting to be in, the chance to make a difference and change the norm of the industry. This entire discussion has reviewed and evaluated, what is involved in forming and maintaining a business. While the primary focus was on the field of business, marketing, and technology; combined with in-depth personal stories. All these fields are interconnected in the operations of a business.

It all begins with developing the business. With the business name set and legal framework determined it allows for the focus of the four prominent areas of business. While the first prominent area focuses on the financial aspect of the business. The financial lens looks at ways to diminish debt and realistic actions to avoid borrowing money while increasing revenue through profit centers. The second area fosters the examination of the industry, diving into the offerings of competitors and processes of the industry. While the final area promotes the importance of values and ethics within the business. Together the four areas solidify the business's foundation, allowing for the expansion of marketing.

While marketing is often the smallest portion of the business's budget, there's a general guideline of the 4 Ps which is the most direct way to approach marketing options. There's a vast array of options to choose from, many of these options do not cost a penny, while others come at a premium. Either option will require time to put together a plan and maintain the information. The use of the internet is a fantastic direction to evaluate.

Though the business continues to grow and expand, technology is ever more affecting the field. Whether it is simply using technology in the business or adopting new technology it is all over the place. Just remember technology has a cost, both monetary and emotional.

Ultimately, the business is at the service of the client.

ABOUT THE AUTHOR

Brandon Sims has over ten years of managerial and operational leadership with a focus in customer relations and research and development. Since 2012, Brandon has been Director of Technology and R&D at New Post Golf Range. Most notably in May 2019, Brandon was featured in the GRAA Magazine for an article entitled "Tech Talk: A stand-alone range in Virginia employs a Director of Technology and R&D...should you?". To this day Brandon continues to grow and pursue a better implementation of technology in the field of business.

Made in the USA
Columbia, SC
12 March 2022